BUG LIFE CYCLES

By Rod Barkman

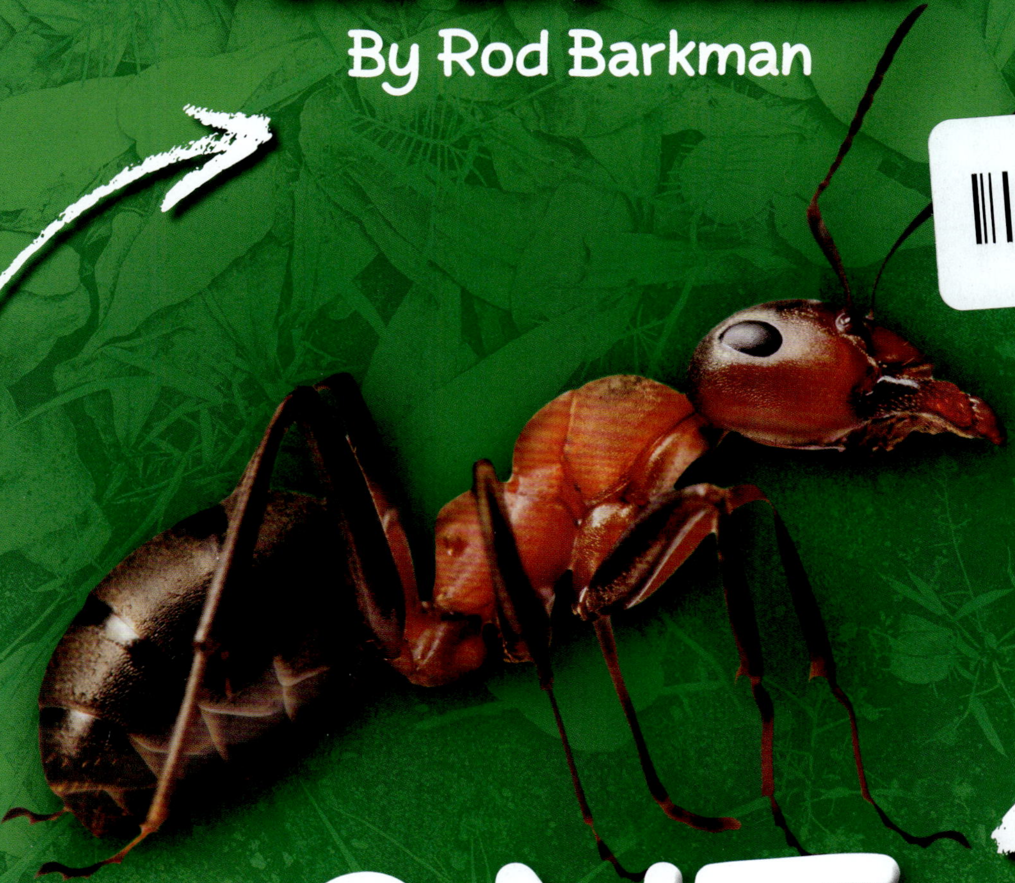

ANT

KidHaven PUBLISHING

Published in 2027 by
KidHaven Publishing, an Imprint of Greenhaven Publishing, LLC
2544 Clinton St., Buffalo, NY 14224

Written by: Rod Barkman
Edited by: Noah Leatherland
Designed by: Amelia Harris

Cataloging-in-Publication Data

Names: Barkman, Rod.
Title: Ant / Rod Barkman.
Description: Buffalo, NY : KidHaven Publishing, 2027. | Series: Bug life cycles | Includes glossary and index.
Identifiers: ISBN 9781534571099 (pbk.) | ISBN 9781534571105 (library bound) | ISBN 9781534571112 (ebook)
Subjects: LCSH: Ants--Juvenile literature. | Ants--Life cycles--Juvenile literature.
Classification: LCC QL568.F7 B37 2027 | DDC 595.796--dc23

Printed in China

CPSIA compliance information: Batch #QS27KH: For further information contact Greenhaven Publishing LLC at 1-844-317-7404.

PHOTO CREDITS
All images are courtesy of Shutterstock.com, unless otherwise stated.

Cover – Andrey Pavlov, Evangelita, Anastasiia Hevko. 2–3 – Long Life. 4–5 – PixieMe, Krakenimages.com, aleks333, Arlette Lopez, logoboom. 6–7 – J. Photos, Darkdiamond67. 8–9 – Garna Zarina, beebatch_photography. 10–11 – Bokeh Blur Background, Dr Morley Read. 12–13 – Hartmut Goldhahn, IanRedding. 14–15 – Pavel Krasensky, sruilk. 16–17 – Dinar Budiman, schankz. 18–19 – Somyot Mali-ngam, Tri_Visuals, corlaffra, CC BY-SA 2.0 < https://commons.wikimedia.org/wiki/File:Exploding_Ant_(Camponotus_(Colobopsis)_cylindricus)_(14914027244).jpg> via Wikimedia Commons. 20–21 – Istiyono, Victor Suarez Naranjo. 22–23 – ploypemuk, Henrik Larsson, siraphat, Hartmut Goldhahn, Kurit afshen.

CONTENTS

Words that look like <u>this</u> can be found in the glossary on page 24.

WHAT IS A LIFE CYCLE?

All living things have a life cycle. A life cycle is the different stages of life that living things go through, from the start to the end of their lives. A life cycle includes aging, having babies, and death.

The human life cycle begins with a baby. The baby grows into a toddler and then a child. The child grows into a teenager, then an adult. Eventually, they become an elderly person.

TEENAGER

ADULT

ELDERLY

MEET THE ANT

Ants are insects. An ant has three main parts to its body—the head, thorax, and abdomen. Like all insects, an ant has six legs. Ants also have antennae and mandibles.

Ants can be found almost everywhere in the world. Only Antarctica, Greenland, and a few other nations do not have their own populations of ants. Ants live in groups called colonies. Colonies are home to different types of ants—queens, workers, and males.

EGG

The ant's life cycle begins with an egg. The queen ant usually lays all the eggs in the colony. The queen ant can lay hundreds or even thousands of eggs a day.

Ant eggs that have been fertilized become female worker ants. Most of the eggs that hatch in a colony become female worker ants. The unfertilized eggs become male ants.

LARVA

Young ants that hatch from eggs are called larvae. Larvae do not have legs or eyes yet. They rely on adult worker ants to bring them food.

Ant larvae molt several times, which means they shed their skin as they grow. As they molt, the larvae grow small hairs. This makes it easier for worker ants to carry them.

PUPA

When the ant larvae are big enough, they form a soft white case around themselves. This case is called a cocoon. Inside these cocoons, the ant larvae slowly change. This is called the pupal stage.

ANT CARRYING A PUPA

During the pupal stage, the ant changes color and becomes darker. By the time it leaves the cocoon, it is a fully-grown adult ant.

ADULT

When the adult ant first breaks out of the cocoon, it tends to the queen ant, the eggs, and the larvae. As worker ants get older, their jobs in the colony often change.

ANTS MOVING A PUPA

Older worker ants usually do more dangerous jobs than younger worker ants. This includes leaving the nest to search for food and protecting the nest from attacks.

Different ants within the colony can be different sizes depending on what job they have.

HOW ANTS LIVE

Every ant in the colony has a job. The queen ant stays in the nest making more eggs. The male ants mate with the queen. They do not live as long as female ants.

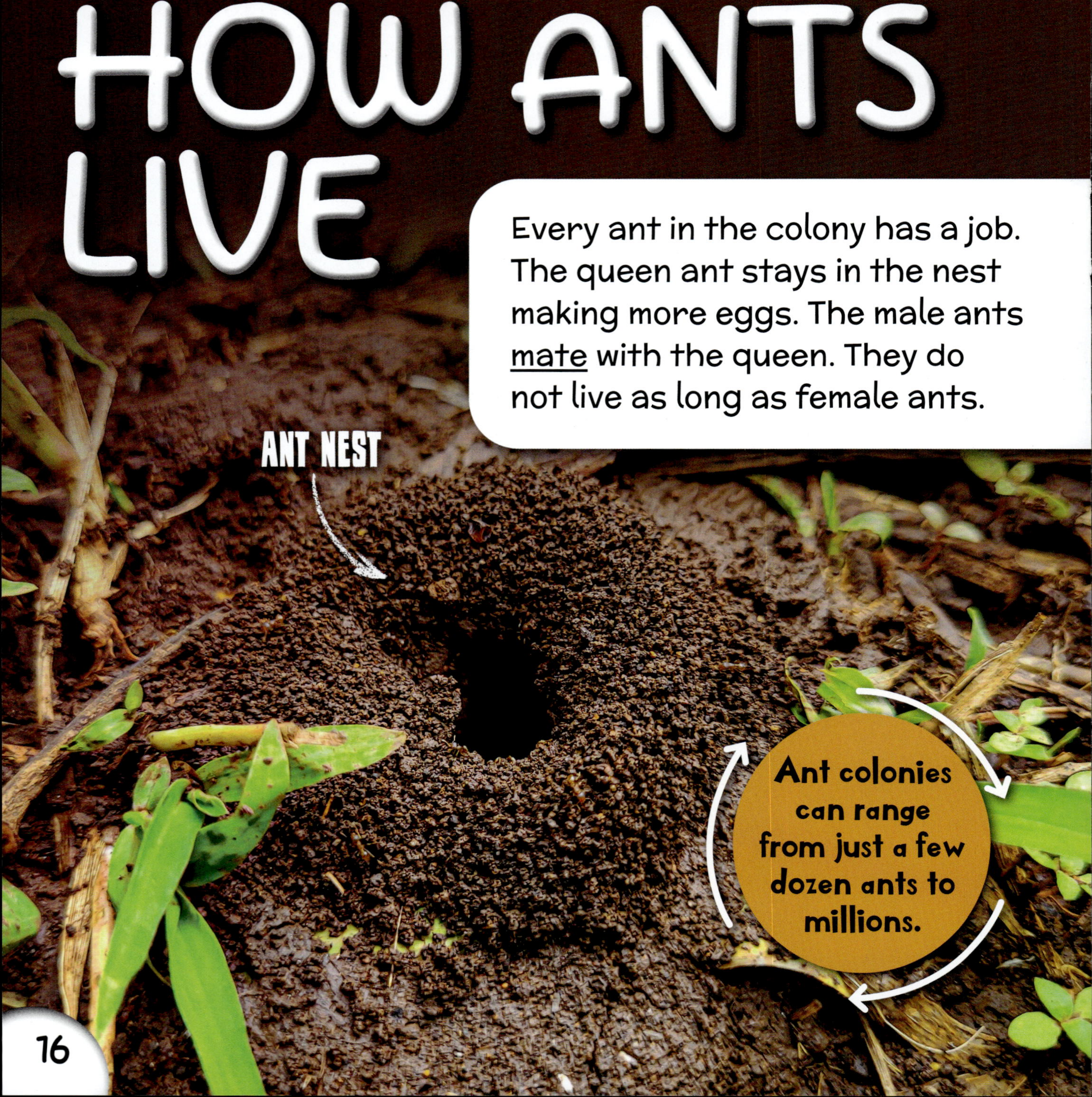

Ant colonies can range from just a few dozen ants to millions.

Some ants emerge with wings. Some are male, and some are female. These ants fly away from the colony they were born in so they can mate with other ants. This allows them to create new colonies.

TYPES OF ANTS

There are over 12,000 known species of ants. Each species is interesting!

FIRE ANTS

hold onto each other to float and survive floods

WEAVER ANTS

weave plants together to make living nests

LEAF-CUTTER ANTS

grow fungus gardens in their nests

EXPLODING ANTS

protect their colony by tearing themselves apart to release a <u>toxic</u> liquid

END OF LIFE

Like all living things, an ant's life comes to an end eventually. This may be because of predators, old age, or even a battle with other ant colonies.

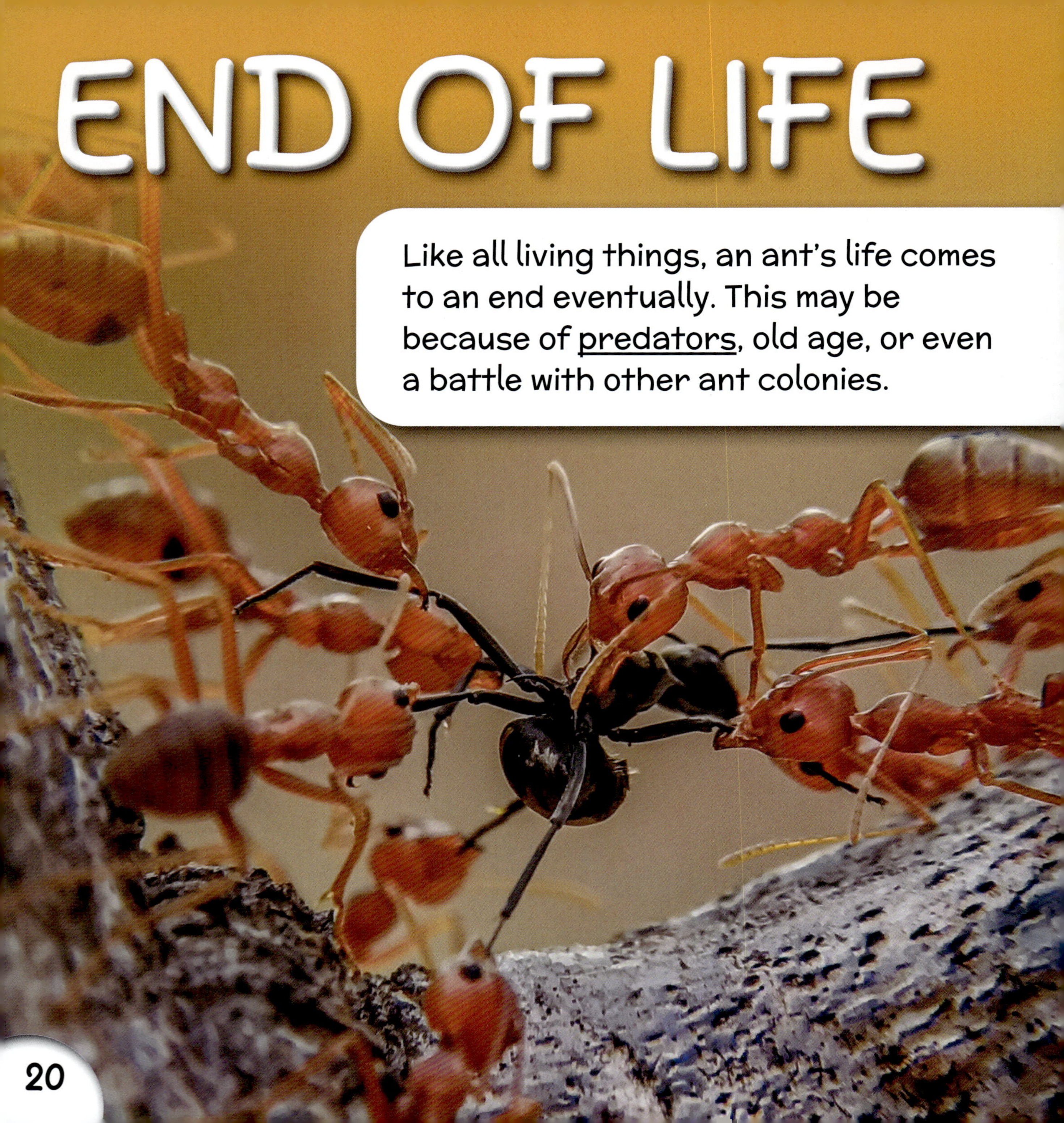

Ant lives can be very short, but some ants can live for years. Even though the ant may die, if their colony has a queen laying eggs, the life cycle continues.

LIFE CYCLE OF AN ANT

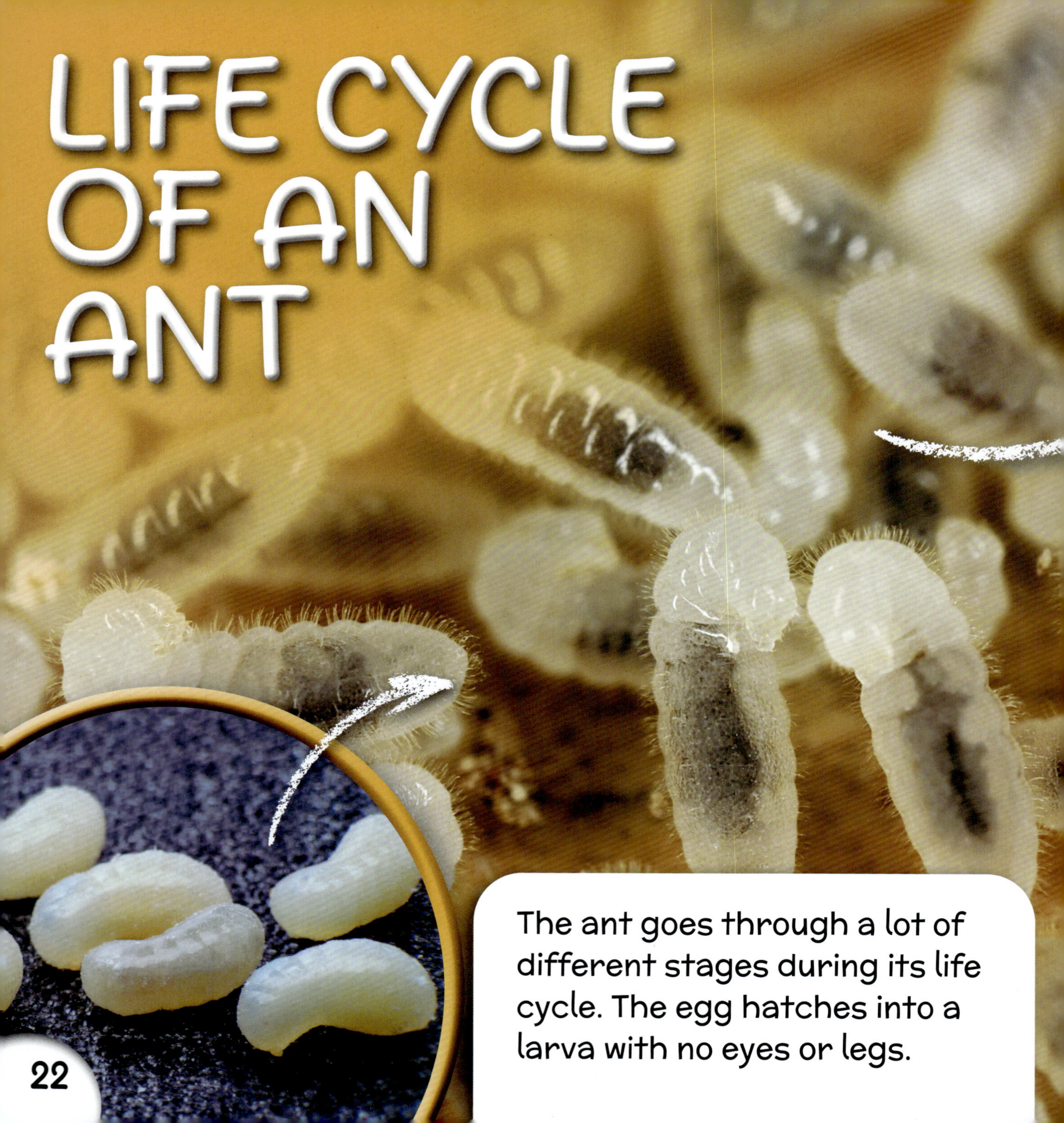

The ant goes through a lot of different stages during its life cycle. The egg hatches into a larva with no eyes or legs.

The larva is fed by worker ants and molts as it grows to maturity. The mature larva spins a cocoon and becomes an adult.

GLOSSARY

antennae long, thin parts of an insect that are used to sense the world

emerge to become visible by coming out or away from something

fertilized to do with eggs that have been changed by material from the male of the species

hatch to break out of an egg

mandibles the jaw-like part of an insect used to bite, grip, or eat

mate to produce young with an animal of the same species

predators animals that hunt other animals for food

species a group of very similar animals or plants that can make babies together

toxic harmful to people, animals, or the world

INDEX